The Case for Using Layered Defenses to Stop Worms

I0411566

Network Architecture and Applications Division
of the
Systems and Network Attack Center (SNAC)

Information Assurance Directorate

David J. Albanese
Michael J. Wiacek
Christopher M. Salter
Jeffrey A. Six

June 18, 2004
Version 1.0

National Security Agency
9800 Savage Rd. STE 6704
Ft. Meade, MD 20755-6704

malcodeteam@nsa.gov

1 Motivation

Internet worms are perceived to be one of the primary threats to the nation's information technology infrastructure. They are a significant cause for concern from both financial and network security perspectives. According to the Worm Information Center FAQ [1], the Sobig and Blaster worms, which occurred at the same time, are estimated to have cost companies more than two billion dollars.

For this paper, we studied current worm strategies and implementations and tried to determine whether the trends point to a significant worsening of the problem in the near future. Are worm technologies improving? Are worm attacks becoming more sophisticated? We were also interested in defensive technologies that can be used to combat the worm problem. Where are defensive technologies best applied? Should other technologies be developed to help defend against the worm problem? Ultimately, we would like to know whether a sophisticated attack can be prevented – could current defensive mechanisms be used to defend against future sophisticated attacks?

2 Paper Organization

Answering our questions required an understanding of current worm technology and how it is evolving. We choose to focus on the technology used by worms rather than the social engineering methods used to deploy them, for which there is no technical solution.

In the **Worm Technology** section (sec. 4) of this paper, we devise a novel method for describing Internet worms based on characteristics they exhibit, which we call *life functions*. By decomposing these life functions, we derived the fundamental conditions needed for worm success, which we call its *attack attributes*. In the **Attack Attributes** section (sec. 5), we describe a system by which to classify worms.

The **Defensive Mechanisms and Techniques** section (sec. 6) surveys the existing technologies that combat worms and other malicious code. The worm *attack attributes* are matched against the defenses in the **Attacks vs. Defenses** section (sec. 7) in a *defense matrix*. From this matrix, we draw conclusions about how best to detect and prevent worm attacks. We present a summary of our results in the **Findings** section (sec. 3) below.

Finally, in the **Applying Defensive Methodology** section (sec. 8), we discuss how five aggressive worms would have been easily defeated using the defense-in-depth strategy that we advocate in this paper.

3 Findings

3.1 Defense-in-Depth

Many defensive technologies have been developed to combat the spread of Internet worms. Unfortunately, there is no single technology that protects against all types of mobile malicious code. Many enterprises rely on only a small set of protective technologies to protect their assets, such as firewalls and virus scanners. Our research suggests that a layered defensive solution would be more effective at preventing all known worm infection vectors and, potentially, many unknown ones as well.

We reached this conclusion based on our study of a wide variety of Internet worms and defensive mechanisms. As part of our research, we have produced a system for describing worms and measuring whether defenses can stop them. We believe that this method captures the critical characteristics that define current worms and the characteristics that will be displayed by worms in the future. Our system demonstrates that no single defense works against all worms and that multiple layered defenses provide robust protection.

Defense-in-depth security helps defend against not only worms but other network threats like Trojan horses, malicious insiders, and hackers who have guessed passwords or entered systems via flaws in network code. It bolsters security with solutions that are effective even without forward knowledge of any attack. Such security solutions scale even to zero-day attacks, which are attacks that make use of previously unknown vulnerabilities. Reactive defenses, like signature-based virus scanners and automated patching systems are still necessary, but they are ineffective against fast moving worms or zero-day attacks.

Worms have increasingly become "blended threats"[12]; they use many different methods to attack systems. In effect, they are using an attack-in-depth strategy in order to carry out their mission. Single-point solutions may be able to block a few of the attack vectors, but will not be able to stop all of them.

3.2 What We Did

Our methodology involves studying some of the most prolific, damaging, and technically sophisticated worms of the past few years. We develop a method of classifying worms based on characteristics they exhibit, which we call *life functions*. From these characteristics, we generated a large set of *attack attributes*, which represent classes of actions taken by worms to ensure successful infection, survival, and propagation. The attack attributes are matched against defensive technologies and presented in a *defense matrix*.

The matrix reveals that certain defensive mechanisms work best against particular worm life functions. But to achieve the best and broadest coverage against the Internet worm threat only a defense-in-depth approach will suffice. Specifically, traditional perimeter defenses, such as firewalls, should be supplemented with host-based protection systems.

Our research distilled worm attacks into their basic building blocks. We reviewed over 30 worms and noted what conditions and actions they need to succeed. In all, we observed over 200 distinct conditions in our sample set of worms. We were able coalesce these conditions into 14 broad categories, which we call worm attack attributes. We believe that by blocking these fourteen attack attributes we can control worms.

We show how well eleven common defenses combat the worm problem by aligning them against the attack attributes in a defense matrix. The matrix, with attack attributes on one axis and defenses on the other, shows whether a defense offers hope toward observing or defending that attack point. A notation at an intersection implies that some protection is afforded against the attribute.

The defense matrix appears in Table 1. A detailed version of the matrix and an in-depth description of our annotation decisions are in the **Attacks vs. Defenses** section (sec. 7).

Attack Attributes / Defenses	Packet Filtering FW	Stateful FW	Application Proxy FW	IDS	Host FW	VM	Configuration	AV with Heuristics	HIPS	Integrity Check	Stackguarding
Exploits vulnerable network code (infection)	X	X	X	X	X		X				X
Tricks a user (infection)			X		X		X				
Exploits vulnerable configuration (infection)	X	X	X		X		X				
Exploits previously installed backdoor (infection)	X	X	X		X			X			
Changes file system							X		X	X	
Changes system settings							X		X	X	
Modifies some process							X		X		
Accesses the network	X	X	X		X				X		
Requires system privilege							X		X		X
Performs anomalous queries							X		X		
Invokes crucial APIs						X			X		
Causes network flooding	X	X	X		X				X		
Slows local system									X		
Contains worm signatures			X	X				X			

Table 1 – Defense Matrix

The first four attack attributes in the defense matrix correspond to the first stage of the worm lifecycle, which we call its infection life function. This is where the worm gains initial control of the system and first executes its code. The remaining attributes can apply to any of the subsequent life stages of worms, be it survival, propagation, or payload. The matrix indicates that certain defenses are most effective at blocking infection while others are better against later life stages.

Most defensive mechanisms used today focus on preventing the initial worm infection. A strong firewall configuration or stackguarding are effective techniques in this regard. Unfortunately, as we can see in the matrix, they are not sufficient. The majority of the worms in our sample set infected machines as a result of a user directly executing the worm (i.e. by clicking on it). Firewalls alone cannot address this infection mechanism since they cannot block all means by which files enter systems. It is unrealistic to assume that users will become cautious about running unknown files.

We must assume that worms will be able to bypass perimeter defenses and continue to get control of systems, as they have for the last 15 years. For this reason, defenses must be geared to block worms in their later life stages. During the survival, propagation, and payload stages, worms generally need to perform actions directly on the infected host. Protections nestled close to the host are better suited to defend against these worm actions. Only these defenses are granular enough to understand the operating system resources being used by the worm.

The defense matrix shows that host-based intrusion prevention systems and strong configuration can detect or combat twelve of our fourteen attack attributes. Host-based intrusion prevention systems offer the most protection against a worm's later life stages. They enforce behavioral policy on a per application basis. This policy enforcement is a critical component of our defense strategy because nearly all worms exhibit anomalous behavior when compared to a baseline of normal system operation. For example, they access resources that should only be touched during program installation or access resources associated with network communication in anomalous ways. Tools that provide protection against the later life stages coupled with tools that prevent initial infection leave no attack attribute that cannot be defended against.

3.3 The State of Worms

This project provided us with insight into the state of worm technology. During this study, we decomposed a wide sample of worms and studied their behaviors. From this, we hoped to be able to assess their sophistication and project the future in worm technology. From the rate at which worms appear across the globe and from the press coverage given them, one would be led to believe that the worm problem is out of control and we are defenseless against it. While there are many worms that have had widespread success, we concluded that they do not exhibit any behaviors that are not addressed by commonly available defenses. Unfortunately, administrators often only deploy defenses that tend to be reactive and do not adequately address all aspects of the problem.

We have observed some advances in the state of worm technologies. We have seen fast spreading worms, highly destructive worms, specially targeted worms, remotely controlled worms, and heavily armored worms (that are hard to analyze). On the surface, these aspects seem very advanced, but upon deeper review, their degree of sophistication has not made huge leaps; it is merely tracking the technology that is available. Once new technology, such as peer-to-peer networks becomes available, worm writers make use of it for spreading and controlling worms.

If sophisticated adversaries were writing worms, then we would expect to see more worms that exploit flaws not known to the public. The small number of such worms suggests that worm writers merely make use of vulnerabilities posted to the Internet to drive infection. Our findings confirm this. The worms that are universally considered to be the most sophisticated are not those that have exhibited the most advanced individual techniques, such as being remotely controlled; they are the ones that have most effectively incorporated all of the various aspects of worms (remotely controlled, fast spreading, specially targeted, and so on). The Leave worm, for instance, used multiple infection vectors, was difficult to analyze, used advanced command and control channels that tunneled through firewalls, and enabled a remotely controllable agent on each target. Our case studies show that the various life stages of Leave and other worms can be prevented by layered defenses.

4 Worm Technology

Many different worms have appeared on the Internet in the past few years. It is infeasible to study all of them, so we selected a subset of worms that we hope covers the entire domain of mobile malicious code. Using this subset, we developed a method to describe comprehensively these common characteristics, which we call their *life functions*. This method is useful for not only describing current worms, but future worms as well.

We describe the types of data we collected to perform this study in the **Worm Analysis** section below. The sample worms we chose are listed in the **Selected Worms** section and our mechanism for describing worms is explained in the **Classifying Worms** and **Life Functions** sections.

4.1 Worm Analysis

Our analysis only considers worms as described by Nazario, et al. [28], rather than other types of viral code. The distinction between worms and viruses is rapidly becoming more blurred, but we still believe that a software component that has the capability to infect other systems in an automated fashion is best described as a worm. We acknowledge that worms may also be activated by non-automated means. In either case, the defensive measures we propose defend against worms and viruses, as well as other types of malicious code.

We collected information on thirty different worms seen on the Internet over the past couple of years. Most of the data came from anti-virus vendor write-ups that are posted on their websites [2-9]. The remainder of the data was obtained from other researchers' work on individual worms [13-22] and from our own independent research.

We focused on collecting information that would answer the following questions:
- What types of vulnerabilities does the worm exploit?
- How fast does the worm spread?
- How does the worm avoid detection?
- Does the worm have a remote command and control capability?
- What requirements or conditions are needed for the worm's success?
- How difficult was the worm to analyze?
- How complicated was the code?
- What residue is left behind when the worm infects a system?
- Does the worm cause any noticeable side effects?

4.2 Selected Worms

For our subset of worms, we chose examples that would be representative of the mobile malicious code space. We selected worms that were the most successful in propagation, technically novel or sophisticated, or most damaging to network infrastructure. By choosing this set of current worms, we expect to be able to predict the advances future worms may make. Below is the list of worms we selected with a brief description of why they were chosen:

BADTRANS – Win32 worm that spreads using Message Application Program Interface (MAPI) commands. It sends out user information, passwords, and log of keystrokes.

BLASTER/LOVSAN/MSBLAST [16]- Win32 worm that exploits the MS RPC DCOM Buffer Overflow. It attempted a distributed denial of service attack (DDOS) against the Microsoft site that distributes software fixes to vulnerabilities (windowsupdate.com).

BUGBEAR/TANATOS [17] – Similar to BADTRANS, but has some additional capabilities. It disables anti-virus software and spreads through network shares and sends traffic to network printers. It also has protection mechanisms such as UPX compression and a polymorphic file infector.

CODERED [13,15] – Win32 worm that attacks the Microsoft Windows WWW server IIS (Internet Information Services). It was one of the first worms to receive attention outside of the network security community because of its speed and effectivness in spreading.

DUMARU – Win32 worm that infects all .EXE files in the root drives of the infected system using alternate data streams to store the virus. It contains its own SMTP engine, and appears to the user as a Microsoft patch.

ETAP/SIMILE [18] – Cross-platform worm that infects both Windows Portable Executable (PE) and Linux Executable and Linkable Format (ELF) executables. Uses an entry-point obscuring technique and a sophisticated polymorphic file infector to avoid detection by anti-virus programs.

FRETHEM – Win32 worm that downloads commands from a website to modify its behavior. It uses its own SMTP engine and social engineering techniques to capture users names and passwords.

GIBE/SWEN [19] – Win32 worm that via an email that appears to the user as a Microsoft security patch.

HLLW.CAKE – Win32 worm that spreads through multiple peer-to-peer networks, including KaZaA, Grokster, and iMesh. It is protected by tElock anti-tamper compression.

JONBARR/PEPEX – Mass-mailing worm that uses its own SMTP engine to send email that pretends to be a Microsoft patch. It also spreads through various peer-to-peer networks, including KaZaA, eDonkey2000, Morpheus, and mIRC.

KLEZ [20]- A widespread Win32 worm that spoofs real email addresses, disables anti-virus software, and infects compressed files. It pretends to be an anti-virus patch against itself.

LION [21] – Linux worm that speads by using a known flaw in BIND.

LEAVE – Win32 worm that uses a previously existing backdoor to infect systems. It uses multiple, encrypted Command and Control channels.

LOVELETTER/ILOVEYOU – Visual Basic email worm that uses very effective social engineering.

MAGISTR – Win32 worm with a malicious payload that erases an infected system's BIOS and hard drive sectors. It uses sophisticated protection and anti-debugging mechanisms and disables the Zone Alarm personal firewall.

MIMAIL – Very effective Win32 mass-mailing worm that scans user files for potential targets and uses a number of different exploits as its payload.

8

MEXER.D – Win32 worm that spreads through multiple peer-to-peer networks, including KaZaA and iMesh. It also attempts to download its payload from a hard-coded website.

MYPARTY – Win32 mass-mailing worm that drops a trojan backdoor onto an infected system.

NIMDA – Sophisticated, fast-spreading Win32 worm that uses both client and server infection vectors.

NACHI – Win32 worm that uses the same exploit as the Blaster worm to remove Blaster infections and patch vulnerable systems.

NEROMA – Visual Basic worm that uses Outlook to send a 9/11-related message (it used that date in its infected message header).

RECORY- Win32 worm that installs itself into local filesystem and propagates by pretending to be an anti-virus tool.

RAMEN [22] - Linux worm that bundles together a number of known exploits against Linux services, including: Wuftp. LPRng, and rpc.statd.

REPAD – Win32 worm that spread through KaZaA network.

SOBIG.F – Win32 worm that harvests email addresses from infected machines and is believed to use spamming techniques to spread using its own SMTP engine. It attempts to download code from a set of machines at a predetermined time.

SLAMMER [31] – Win32 worm that exploits a flaw in Microsoft's SQL Server and spread. It spread very quickly, infecting 90% of vulnerable machines within 10 minutes.

SPIDA – A JavaScript worm that uses weak default usernames and passwords to compromise sytems running Microsoft SQL server.

STRANO – Malicious code that spreads by IRC channels and infecting Word documents.

VOTE.K – Destructive mass-mailing worm written in Visual Basic. Uses the Outlook Express addressbook and KaZaA to spread.

YAHA – A prolific mass-mailing Win32 worm that disables anti-virus programs and personal firewalls.

4.3 Classifying Worms

We wanted a simple way to describe worms according to their common characteristics. The characteristics we were most interested in are those that would allow a defensive mechanism to detect and/or prevent the worm. To our knowledge, worm behavior had not been previously described with a focus on the defensible conditions exhibited.

Nazario, et al. [28], decompose worm functions using six general characteristics. We believe that worms possess another capability important for defense which they do not discuss. This is the ability of a worm to survive on a system and remain undetected. It is important for a defensive mechanism to be able to determine if worm code has a foothold on a system and prevent it from doing any harm.

Singh [29] also decomposes worm behavior into six categories, which he calls "organs" to coincide with his biological analogy. His approach uses Visual Basic examples to describe both virus and worm behaviors. While his categorization is comprehensive, it is too complex for our purposes.

Our method of describing Internet worms uses only the most basic characteristics that worms exhibit. We note the requirements necessary for the worms to gain control of a host, maintain that control, propagate to other hosts, and execute a payload. All worms fulfill the first three requirements, and most fulfill the last. We describe in detail examples of each of these requirements in the **Life Functions** section below.

4.4 Life Functions

In this section we decompose worms into the basic life functions they perform. For each function, we cover the currently used techniques, highlighting any advances. This should lend perspective to the state of worms and how to ultimately defend against them. We believe that we can classify any worm according to the following functions:

- Infection
- Survival
- Propagation
- Payload

4.4.1 Infection

Infection refers to how a worm gains initial control of a system.

4.4.1.1 Types of Infection Vectors

Worms rely on two general methods to infect a host. Either they exploit a flaw in software running on a system, or they are the result of some action taken by a user. After studying details from our set of worms, we have been able to identify four distinct categories of infection vectors. They are:

- An exploitable portion of network aware code
- A vulnerable configuration of a network aware component
- A user's action
- An existing system backdoor

4.4.1.1.1 An Exploitable Portion of Network Aware Code

Buffer overflows are the most commonly found vulnerability in network aware code. They exist when a program accepts more input data than it is prepared to store. In such a case, the input overflows other parts of memory, overwriting other essential program data. If the overwritten data controls program flow, such as return addresses or function pointers, an attacker may be able to specially format his input in order to remotely execute instructions on the system by altering this control information. It is important to keep in mind that in order to exploit such an overflow condition, an attacker must be able to control input to the vulnerable program. After gaining control in this manner, the exploiting code runs with the same privileges as the exploited code. Thus the most valuable buffer overflow to an attacker is one found in a program that accepts input from the network and runs in a privileged context such as Administrator, SYSTEM, or root. Unfortunately, many of the network services on modern operating systems run at high privilege levels.

In addition to buffer overflows, there are a number of other programming flaws that could potentially lead to exploitable vulnerabilities. These include logic errors in file directory traversal functions, uninitialized variables, errors in ASCII to Unicode (and Unicode to ASCII) conversion routines, race conditions, signed/unsigned comparison errors, and off-by-one errors. But because they are more difficult to find, analyze, and exploit, these other vulnerabilities have not been exploited by worm writers to nearly the extent that buffer overflows have been. If buffer overflows were made more difficult to exploit, using countermeasures such as stackguarding, it is likely worm authors would need to begin exploiting other, more challenging vulnerabilities. A potential result of this evolution is that we would see fewer worms, but at the same time, they would be much more sophisticated and possibly dangerous.

4.4.1.1.2 A Vulnerable Configuration of a Network Aware Component

Even if a network service is carefully programmed, it can still be exploitable if it is not set up properly. The Spida worm took advantage of a weak default configuration of the SQL Server database application. The default configuration contained a privileged account that had no password. Spida connected to machines that were running SQL Server and attempted to login using this account. Unless an administrator had specifically disabled this account, the worm could gain control of that system at a high privilege level.

4.4.1.1.3 A User's Action

A large number of the worms studied by the team did not propagate through vulnerabilities; rather they relied on a distinct user action for initial infection. In this case, the user usually receives a program via email and is tricked into believing it is something else, such as a game, a screensaver, or digital photographs from a party. Since this infection technique relies on actions outside of the attacker's control, it is less reliable and such a worm propagates more slowly than purely automated approaches that require no user action.

4.4.1.1.4 An Existing Backdoor

Some worms exploit "backdoors" left by previous security breaches. A backdoor is a mechanism that is created by a computer program that allows anyone with knowledge of its existence to gain some control over the system. The Leave worm infected systems that already had a SubSeven backdoor installed. Properly updated anti-virus tools should have been capable of detecting SubSeven and removing it, thereby closing the backdoor. This would have made people immune to a network-based Leave infection.

4.4.1.2 Attributes Associated with Infection

Table 2, below, outlines the vulnerabilities that selected worms depend on for successful infection. Many worms exploit known vulnerabilities while others require user action in order to get control of the system.

Vulnerability or Action Required	Worms
MS00-052 – Registry-Invoked Programs Use Standard Search Path	CODERED
MS00-078 – Patch for 'Web Server Folder Traversal' Vulnerability	NIMDA
MS01-020 – Incorrect MIME Header Can Cause IE to execute Email Attachment	BADTRANS, FRETHEM, YAHA, NIMDA, BUGBEAR
MS01-033 – Unchecked Buffer in Index Server ISAPI Extension Could Enable Web Server Compromise	CODERED
MS01-044 – 15 August 2001 Cumulative Patch for IIS	NIMDA
MS03-014 – April 2003 Cumulative Patch for Outlook Express	MIMAIL
MS02-015 – 28 March Cumulative Patch for Internet Explorer	MIMAIL
MS02-039 – Buffer Overruns in SQL Server 2000 Resolution Service Might Enable Code Execution	SLAMMER
MS03-007 – Unchecked Buffer in Windows Component May Cause Web Server Compromise	NACHI
MS03-026 – Buffer Overrun in RPC May Allow Code Execution	BLASTER, NACHI
Microsoft advisory Q313418 – Unsecured SQL Server password	SPIDA
Preexisting SubSeven infection	LEAVE
VU-196945 – ISC Bind 8 Buffer Overflow in Transaction Signature (TSIG) Handling Code	LION
VU # 29823, VU # 34043, VU # 382365: Multiple Format String Errors	RAMEN
VU # 102795 - Buffer Overflows in OpenSSL Servers	SLAPPER
User Runs Infected File	DUMARU, ETAP, FRETHEM, GIBE, HLLW.CAKE, JONBARR, KLEZ, LEAVE, LOVELETTER, MAGISTR, MEXER, MYPARTY, NEROMA, REPAD, SOBIG, STRANO, VOTE.K

Table 2 – Vulnerability Based Infection Vectors

4.4.1.3 State of Infection Vectors

One of the few worms to use a zero-day exploit was the classic Morris worm of 1988 (the first known worm). Almost all worms in the past fifteen years have exploited publicly known vulnerabilities or tricked the user into executing them. This study did not uncover any evidence of a change or impending change in the sophistication of infection vectors. While some vulnerabilities clearly require more skill than others to exploit (a mass mailing worm is much easier to develop than one that exploits a buffer overflow), the types of infection vectors appear to be fairly stable. Some advanced worms use combinations of these standard vectors to increase their effectiveness. We believe that we will see more of these worms, such as Nimda, that are capable of infecting hosts in a number of ways.

In general, system administrators cannot be relied upon to install patches and users cannot be counted on to refrain from running programs that they receive via email. The lack of evolution with regard to infection vectors can be attributed to one overarching cause, the sheer effectiveness that worm authors have (and continue to have) in exploiting publicly known vulnerabilities and in tricking users into executing their code.

4.4.2 Survival

The survival life function describes how a worm maintains control over a host once it has penetrated the host's defenses. This category includes the following behaviors:

- Resuming execution at a later time
- Evading detection
- Disabling detection software
- Preventing decompilation or reverse-engineering

4.4.2.1 Resuming Execution at a Later Time

One of the first actions taken by most worms is to install some mechanism to ensure that it will execute again at a later time. This mechanism is primarily used to ensure worm survivability between reboots, but it has other uses as well – it can be used to execute some of the worm code in response to an action that has occurred on the infected system. For example, some worms might launch their payload code at a specified time or might propagate when a user sends an email message.

There are a number of different strategies used by worms to ensure that they can regain control at a later time. Many worms will use a combination of these techniques to ensure the greatest chance of survival:

- Modify startup files
- Use a job scheduling utility
- File infection or replacement
- Registry changes (on Microsoft Windows systems)
- Changing file-type handler

4.4.2.1.1 Modify Startup Files

These files control the startup of the operating system (or some component of it). Worms may insert instructions into these files to launch themselves on subsequent reboots. Files often targeted by worms include:

- system.ini, win.ini, etc. for Windows
- /etc/rc.d/rc.sysinit, etc. for Linux

4.4.2.1.2 Job Scheduling Utility

Some worms schedule themselves to run on a timed basis, typically known as "cron" job. Typical facilities that can be targeted include:

- AT utility in Windows
- anacron in Linux

4.4.2.1.3 File Infection or Replacement

Some worms inject themselves into binary files or shell scripts, or entirely replace the file with worm code. Any time the altered program is run, the worm gains control of the system.

4.4.2.1.4 Registry Changes

Perhaps the most common way of ensuring that a worm gets to run on a Windows machine is to change one of the "Run" Registry keys. These keys contain lists of programs that the operating system automatically starts. In addition to Run keys, there are many other registry entries that control the launching of programs or services.

4.4.2.1.5 Changing File Type Handler

In Windows (and many windowing systems for Unix/Linux systems), an application can be associated with a file type, determined by its extension (in Windows). A worm could replace the handler for a specific extension (or file type for operating systems that do not determine file type based on extension), so that a double-click or other "open" action on the file causes the worm code to execute.

4.4.2.2 Evading Detection

Evading detection by anti-virus and other defense software is vital to a worm's survivability. Some techniques employed by worms to avoid detection are:

- Employing obfuscation or encryption to avoid being flagged by signature-based scanners.
- Using polymorphic and metamorphic techniques to change themselves in order to avoid defense systems that rely on signature detection.
- Masking outbound traffic so that it looks like normal network traffic in order to avoid detection systems that analyze network traffic.

4.4.2.3 Disabling Detection Software

It is common for malicious code to disable anti-virus software, personal firewalls, or intrusion detection systems. Worms may disable the detection mechanism or modify it so that it does not work properly.

4.4.2.4 Preventing Reverse Engineering

The true purpose and capabilities of new worms cannot be fully understood until they are reverse engineered. Malicious code authors are taking measures to ensure that this cannot be done quickly. This also prevents the quick computation of a signature that can be used by anti-virus software. Reverse engineering prevention measures can be applied to the worm itself or to its payload. Some of the anti-reverse engineering techniques we have seen include:

- Demand-based deobfuscation, where the worm only decrypts portions of code as needed, and re-encrypts these portions when they are no longer needed.
- Anti-debugging techniques employed to detect and foil debuggers.
- Strong encryption where the encryption key is not determinable by examining a copy of the worm.

4.4.3 Attributes Associated with Survival

In table 3 below, we show some of the significant survival attributes. We consider an attribute to be any residue left by worms, any side effect caused them, or any prerequisite for their success.

Survival Attribute	Worms
File System Related	
Creates or modifies files in system directory	BADTRANS, BLASTER, BUGBEAR, FRETHEM, GIBE, HLLW.CAKE, JONBARR, LOVELETTER, MAGISTR, MEXER, MIMAIL, NACHI, NIMDA, RECORY, REPAD, SLAMMER, SPIDA, STRANO, VOKE.K, YAHA
\Documents and Settings\%infected user name%\Start Menu\Programs\Startup	BUGBEAR, GIBE, MYPARTY
system.ini	DUMARU, NEROMA, VOTE.K
win.ini	DUMARU, VOTE.K
Windows Registry Related	
HKLM\SOFTWARE\Microsoft\Windows\CurrentVersion\Run	BLASTER, DUMARU, GIBE, HLLW.CAKE, JONBARR, KLEZ, LEAVE, LOVELETTER, MAGISTR, MEXER, MIMAIL, RECORY, REPAD, SOBIG, STRANO, VOTE.K
HKLM\SOFTWARE\Microsoft\Windows\CurrentVersion\Run Once	BADTRANS, BUGBEAR
Process Related	
Launches processes to aid in propagation	RAMEN, LION
Terminates anti-virus software or host-based firewall	YAHA, BUGBEAR, JONBARR, KLEZ

Table 3 - Significant Survival Attributes

4.4.3.1 Current State of Survival Attribute

An increasing number of worms is now targeting security tools in order to disable them. We have also seen advances in preventing reverse engineering and in avoiding detection. Fortunately, not many worms have been armored with these sophisticated protections. More than half of our sample worms simply placed files in a system directory. Nearly as many modified the Windows Registry's Run keys to make sure they get launched in the future.

4.4.4 Propagation

Propagation vectors come into play when a worm has already established control over a host. They deal with what a worm must do in order to spread itself to other hosts.

4.4.4.1 Types of Propagation

We have identified four primary methods of worm propagation.

- Sending infected email
- Inserting copies onto peer-to-peer (P2P) networks
- Placing copies on file shares
- Scanning for and exploiting remotely vulnerable hosts

4.4.4.1.1 Sending Infected Email

Many worms send themselves as attachments to email messages. Prior to sending such messages, the worms typically gather target addresses from a user's inbox, the local file system, and Registry keys. Such worms may use the infected machine's email program or utilize their own SMTP engine to send email to potential victims. The use of an independent SMTP engine allows worms to propagate independent of the host's email engine. The Frethem, Dumaru, and Yaha worms all contained their own SMTP engines.

4.4.4.1.2 Inserting Copies on Peer-to-Peer (P2P) Networks

A more recent technique for worm propagation is the utilization of peer-to-peer (P2P) networks. P2P software, which enables files to be shared and downloaded from computers directly or indirectly connected to each other, has seen a dramatic increase in popularity. Worms, such as HLLW.Cake and Repad, take advantage of these programs in order to infect other hosts. These worms typically make themselves available on P2P networks under filenames that most users would find enticing. They may disguise themselves as digitally encoded songs, applications, or any other file type that the P2P network allows.

4.4.4.1.3 Placing Copies on File Shares

Worms may also propagate via file shares. A worm places a copy of itself in a directory that is shared with other computers. The worm relies on users on other machines seeing the file and copying it to their local computers, mistaking it for a legitimate file. This method is not very successful for spreading between networks, but can work well when combined with other propagation methods. For example, once a worm has infected a network machine through a mechanism unrelated to file shares, it can utilize file shares as a propagation vector to spread to other machines with the local LAN. Since firewalls typically restrict file sharing at points *between* the local LAN and the Internet, very seldom do firewalls block LAN based file sharing. Bugbear, Nimda, and Gibe used this method to augment their propagation.

4.4.4.1.4 Scanning for and Exploiting Remote Vulnerabilities

This method of propagation involves exploiting a programming or configuration error in software running on a remote system. The worm scans for vulnerable machines and attempts to send them malicious or malformed data in an effort to exploit them. Some worms do not scan for vulnerable machines, they simply assume every host on the Internet is vulnerable and attempt to exploit random IP addresses. Either way, this propagation technique involves a worm using one host that has been compromised to search for and exploit other hosts.

Scanning methods employed by worms can vary. Many worms use random scanning, simply generating an address at random and attempting to infect that host. Some worms have employed a variation of random scanning, favoring addresses that are closer to the host machine, such as those on same subnet. A worm can simply carry around a list of potential targets that is supplied by the worm author or developed through scans of remote systems. Future scanning innovations may also involve coordination between copies of worms, ensuring that machines are only scanned once. An in-depth discussion of various worm scanning methods is covered by Staniford, et al. in [24].

In order to propagate via remote vulnerabilities, worms must copy themselves from the compromised host and onto the network. A common scenario for a worm is to piggyback on an existing service. If a worm uses a network port that is already opened, it has the advantage of being more difficult to filter. For example, worms that use TCP port 80 for communications cannot be blocked at the firewall, as web traffic would also be blocked. Worms such as Slammer that use a port normally utilized by a specific local service can be easily detected and defeated by firewalls and networks that are properly designed and configured.

4.4.4.2 Attributes Associated with Propagation

There are many attributes associated with worm propagation, such as the use of Registry keys and files accessed for target reconnaissance. Other attributes include the modification of processes or the use of ports to facilitate propagation. Some of the significant or more frequently recorded attributes are noted in table 4 below.

Propagation Attribute	Worms
Reconnaissance – Registry Related	
Active Internet Settings Key	GIBE, MAGISTR
\HKCU\Software\Microsoft\Internet Acct Manager\Accounts\00000001\SMTP Server	FRETHEM, MYPARTY
Reconnaissance – File System	
.dbx (Outlook Express email folder)	DUMARU, FRETHEM, MAGISTR, MYPARTY, SOBIG
.wab files (Outlook Address Book)	DUMARU, FRETHEM, KLEZ, MAGISTR, MYPARTY, SOBIG, YAHA
.mbx (Outlook email folder)	FRETHEM, MAGISTR
.eml (Outlook email message)	FRETHEM, SOBIG
.txt (ASCII text file)	KLEZ, SOBIG
htm/.html (HTML file)	JONBARR, KLEZ, SOBIG
ICQ list	KLEZ, YAHA
Network Ports Used	
Port 25/TCP	BADTRANS, DUMARU, FRETHEM, GIBE, JONBARR, KLEZ, MAGISTR, RECORY, YAHA,
Port 27374/TCP	LEAVE, LION
Port 80/tcp	LEAVE, SLAPPER
IRC Ports	LEAVE, LOVELETTER, STRANO
Windows File Shares	BUGBEAR, ETAP

18

Spreading – Mass Mail Engine	
Uses Outlook	RECORY, LOVELETTER, NEROMA, VOTE.K
Uses its own SMTP engine	BUGBEAR, DUMARU, FRETHEM, JONBARR, KLEZ, YAHA

Spreading	
Tries to infect all files on drives C-Z	DUMARU, KLEZ, NIMDA
HKCU\Software\Kazaa\LocalContent	MEXER, RECORY, VOTE.K
\Documents and Settings\%infected user name%\Start Menu\Programs\Startup	GIBE, MYPARTY
Uses network shares	BUGBEAR, KLEZ
Infects Microsoft Word documents with macro virus	STRANO

Spreading – Peer-to-Peer Networks	
Peer-to-Peer Music Networks	GIBE, HLLW.CAKE, JONBARR, RECORY, REPAD
KaZaA	HLLW.CAKE, JONBARR, MEXER, REPAD, VOTE.K
iMesh	HLLW.CAKE, MEXER
\mIRC folder - script.ini	GIBE, VOTE.K, STRANO, JONBARR

Spreading – Server Modifications	
Modifies web content files to infect visiting clients/hosts	NIMDA
Creates IIS Virtual Directories for C & D drives (wide open)	CODERED

Table 4 - Significant Propagation Attributes

4.4.4.3 State of Propagation

A well-designed worm can spread with incredible speed. The Slammer worm is an excellent example of a worm that exploited a vulnerability that specifically lent itself to a fast rate of propagation. Since it, required only a single UDP packet to be sent to a target, Slammer could continuously scan and infect machines without having to wait for a response. Within ten minutes it had infected 90 percent of the vulnerable hosts (at least 75,000) on the Internet [31].
If the available patch for the vulnerability that Slammer exploited had been applied, the number of infected hosts could have been dramatically decreased. Due to the speed of infection, network administrators were unable to respond to the worm in time to stop it.

Typically, a worm's propagation success is based on the quantity of machines infected and how quickly they are infected. In the future, there may be other ways to view success in propagation. A worm may seek to propagate without detection. For example, Badtrans used a 30-second timer for programmed mailings in order to prevent network flooding that would alert administrators. Worms like Badtrans may lead to a new class of propagation techniques that try to fly "under the radar" of network administrators by moving "low and slow."

Targeted propagation, where a worm tries to infect specific machines, is an emerging technique. While none of the observed worms only used targeted propagation, some worms have shown the beginnings of targeted attacks. Spida excluded specific IP addresses from its potential targets. Bugbear featured some early forms of targeted propagation. Bugbear captured network

19

passwords and user's keystrokes and then emailed them to its author if the domain of the system's default email address appeared to be a financial institution. Targeted propagation is likely to develop further as time progresses.

4.4.5 Payload

The payload of a worm is the code or package it carries to perform a task beyond its standard life cycle functions. Not all worms have a payload.

4.4.5.1 Types of Payloads

We have seen four major categories of payloads:

- Establishing backdoor control
- Establishing a distributed denial-of-service agent
- Harvesting information
- Causing destruction

4.4.5.1.1 Establish Backdoor Control

Backdoors are pieces of code that enable remote control of compromised systems. There are a number of different ways used to communicate with these backdoors. Some worms use sharing technologies that are adapted to provide a command and control mechanism such as: file shares (Bugbear and Nimda), P2P networks (Slapper), and IRC (Dumaru). One of the most sophisticated worms to date, Leave, retrieved its encrypted commands from lists downloaded from websites and from private IRC channels.

4.4.5.1.2 Establish a Denial-of-Service Agent

Several worms were designed to create a network of distributed denial-of-service (DDoS) agents. We have seen two types of DDoS payloads. Some with hard coded targets (e.g. Blaster targeted windowsupdate.com), and some that were adaptable (e.g. Leave, which accepted targeting information remotely).

4.4.5.1.3 Harvesting Information

Some worm payloads are designed to harvest information from infected machines. The Lion and Ramen worms copied and exfiltrated password files. Badtrans and Bugbear installed keystroke loggers in order to collect user passwords from electronic commerce and other applications.

4.4.5.1.4 Causing Destruction

The Magistr worm is a good example of a worm with a destructive payload. This worm attempted to overwrite local hard drives and destroy a host's BIOS, rendering the system inoperable and only salvageable by a skilled technician. The Spida worm simply aimed to destroy certain files. This type of payload, where the goal is to destroy compromised systems, appears to be rare and has not been seen very often in the group of worms that we have studied.

4.4.5.2 Attributes Associated with Payloads

We noted various attributes associated with worm payloads. The most significant actions performed or ports used are outlined in table 5 below.

Payload Attribute	Worms
Network Ports Used	
Port 80/TCP (to download backdoor)	FRETHEM, LION
Port 80/TCP (to download commands)	LEAVE
IRC ports	LEAVE, LOVELETTER
Port 27374/TCP/SubSeven (distribution)	LEAVE
Port 1434/UDP (distribution)	SLAMMER
Port 1433/UDP (distribution)	SPIDA
Port 1080/TCP (distribution and backdoor)	BUGBEAR
Port 36794/TCP (finds firewall, etc. And stops)	BUGBEAR
Port 443/TCP (to upload exploit/payload)	SLAPPER
Port 2002/UDP (establish p2p network)	SLAPPER
Port 1978/UDP (establish p2p network)	SLAPPER
Port 4156/UDP (establish p2p network)	SLAPPER
Port 1052/UDP (establish p2p network)	SLAPPER
Collection	
Installs keystroke logger	BADTRANS, BUGBEAR, LOVELETTER
IRC	LEAVE
Emails files to addresses in China	LION, RAMEN
Emails files containing IP address	SPIDA
Emails random files from computer with extensions: mp8,.txt,.htm, html, .wab, .asp, .doc, .rtf, .xls, .jpg, .cpp, .pas, .mpg, mpeg, .bak, .mp3, .pdf	KLEZ
Reconnaissance	
Checks title of currently opened window	BADTRANS
Scans for potential victims using FTP	RAMEN
Destructive	
Overwrites CMOS	MAGISTR
Flashes BIOS	MAGISTR
Destroys Blaster Worm	NACHI
DDoS Payload	BLASTER
Installs rootkit (t0rn)	LION
Trojan system binaries	LION
Provides attacker ability to execute arbitrary commands	LEAVE

21

At predetemined time, connects to hardcoded IPs (20 of them) and downloads and runs a file	SOBIG
Deletes or overwrites files	LOVELETTER, NEROMA, SPIDA, VOTE.K
Shuts down computer	REPAD
Joins P2P potential DDoS network	SLAPPER
Security	
Terminates AV or Firewall	BUGBEAR, JONBARR, KLEZ, YAHA
Removes or modfies TCP wrappers	LION
Kills syslogd	LION
Encrypts files, commands, and/or registry keys	LEAVE
Disables FTP and/or rpc.statd to prevent reinfection	RAMEN
Changes passwords	SPIDA

Table 5 - Payload Attributes

4.4.5.3 State of Worm Payloads

While many worms do not have discernible payloads, those that do can prove effective in significantly disrupting the Internet. We have not seen many destructive payloads, but the ones that we have seen, such as Magistr, are dangerous enough to render compromised hosts inoperable. Equally troubling are those that install backdoors or DDoS agents on systems to pave the way for future coordinated attacks. There does not seem to be a prevailing payload type favored by worm authors. This can be attributed to a wide range of goals that authors have for their worms. Some authors simply want to create worms that spread quickly, some want to capture passwords and other data that they can they utilize, and others want to cause destruction on the hosts that they infect. For as many different motivations a worm author may have, we will likely continue to see as many different payload types.

5 Attack Attributes

Our sample set of worms exhibits common characteristics when carrying out their life functions, as described in the **Worm Technology** section. These characteristics represent specific observable actions taken by worms to ensure their successful infection, survival, and propagation.

We call these characteristics the *attack attributes* of the worm, and we break them down into three basic categories: The first is any condition that exists to allow a successful worm attack, such as a vulnerable network service or an incorrectly configured system. The second category is any observable residue left behind when a worm infects a system, such as a file alteration, changes made to the Windows Registry, or a modified process that is left by the worm. The final category of attack attributes is any behavior caused as a side effect of the worm infection, such as an observable increase in network traffic when the worm attempts to find new targets.

We have identified nearly two hundred detailed attack attributes. We then distilled these attributes into fourteen general attack attributes. We believe that these fourteen categories cover the range of attributes displayed by worms in the past and are very likely to see in worms of the future. Below, we introduce each of the attributes.

5.1 Exploits Vulnerable Network Code

A vulnerability in network-aware code is sometimes a prerequisite for worm infection. The fastest spreading worms have generally exploited network-aware services in an automated fashion. In the set of worms we studied, the most common vulnerability in this class is a buffer overflow condition.

5.2 Tricks the User

Another common infection mechanism is to trick a user into executing the worm itself. The bulk of mass-mailing worms rely on users unwittingly running an infected program by making it appear to be a benign attachment.

5.3 Exploits Vulnerable Configuration

Vulnerable configurations cover a variety of problems beyond flawed code, such as weak password settings, wide-open permissions, and poorly configured trust relationships.

5.4 Exploits Previously Installed Backdoors

A worm uses an existing backdoor on the system to install itself.

5.5 Changes File System

Nearly all worms leave some evidence in the file system. They generally copy themselves to key points in the file system and change configuration files to ensure that they are invoked at a later point in time.

5.6 Changes System Settings

Of the thirty worms studied, seventeen made changes to the Windows Registry. Often this attribute is associated with worm survival, as these modifications are typically made to cause the worm to run automatically.

5.7 Modifies a Process

Some of the more sophisticated worms inject themselves into already running processes. Along with the action of modifying a running process, this attribute includes starting or stopping other processes.

5.8 Accesses the Network

This attribute is evident in worms that propagate over a network or receive commands via a network.

5.9 Requires Advanced Privilege

Worms that need access to restricted resources are only successful if they run with enough privilege to access those resources. Worms that gain initial control by exploiting system services already have such privilege, as do worms that exploit applications that run under a high privilege level. Other worms attempt to verify their current privilege level or seek to increase it.

5.10 Performs Anomalous Queries

Some worms make use of information from the system they have infected. For example, mass-mailers make use of the local system to gather email addresses. This information is often found by searching registry keys and files that are likely to contain such data.

5.11 Invokes Crucial APIs

Worms generally need to perform some crucial action. Mass-mailing worms are likely to invoke the operating system's SMTP APIs in order to propagate further.

5.12 Causes Network Flooding

Aggressively propagating worms may impact available network bandwidth. Administrators noticing a drain on available network bandwidth have used network sniffers to discover a new attack was underway.

5.13 Slows Local System

Worms may impact system response times or cause a large amount of logging activity. This is generally either intentional or as a result of a poorly written worm.

5.14 Contains Worm Signatures

There are a limited number of ways to code worm functionality. Therefore, programs can be examined for coding patterns indicative of older worms in order to notice a new one. Today, most anti-virus software is capable of performing heuristic scanning on files that may indicate the existence of malicious code.

6 Defensive Mechanisms and Techniques

The most common methods used to defend against worms today are reactive, e.g. virus scanning, or software patching. These mechanisms have no hope of preventing fast spreading worms, or worms that use zero-day exploits to carry out their attacks. This is not to say that these technologies are not useful. In fact, they are an essential part of a defense-in-depth strategy.

In this section we identify proactive defensive technologies and mechanisms that can be used to prevent Internet worms today. For this study, we have chosen to only include current technology and do not consider emerging technology, such as techniques aimed at throttling the spread of worms. We also do not consider pure layer 2 and layer 3 (in the OSI model) defense mechanisms, such as Private Virtual Local Area Networks (PVLANs). While both classes of technology clearly have promise as defenses against worms, our analysis concentrates on current, well known, and common techniques and how effective we can be against worms using such technologies.

6.1 Firewalls – Packet Filtering

Packet filters operate on the network and transport layers of the TCP/IP network model. They allow any field in the network or transport headers of a packet to be matched against a set of rules. For example, packets containing specific IP addresses and ports may be blocked. There is no content checking or protocol validation at this level. Packet Filtering is usually implemented with a dedicated firewall or a filtering router.

6.2 Firewalls - Stateful

Stateful firewalls keep track of network connections and monitor their state. Such a firewall identifies requests that were sent from inside the protected network and allow responses to those requests into the network if appropriate. They can filter based on the addresses and ports used by the local or remote host. If a packet is part of an existing connection, it may be allowed, while a similar packet appearing outside of an existing connection would be dropped.

6.3 Firewalls - Application Proxy

The clients and servers never communicate directly when using application proxy firewalls. Firewalls included in this category operate at the application layer of the TCP/IP network model. They enable content checking and validation of the application protocol.

6.4 Intrusion Detection Systems (IDS)

Intrusion Detection Systems (IDS) can best be thought of as a combination virus scanner and network sniffer. Such a system is configured with a database of signatures for known malicious code and suspicious behavior. An IDS monitors all traffic on the network segment to which it is connected and each packet is scanned against the signature database. If a match is found, an administrator can be alerted to the presence of suspicious activity on the network. Some IDSs are sophisticated enough to filter the suspicious traffic or divert it to an isolated location where it can do no harm.

6.5 Host Firewalls

Host firewalls sit on a host between applications on the host and the network. They enforce rules that define the manner in which specific applications may use the network. Such a tool is interested in connections at the network, transport, and application layers of the TCP/IP model and is helpful in thwarting worms that make unusual connections. It is important to keep in mind that a host-based firewall cannot detect malicious activity that appears consistent with a user's normal behavior since these firewalls develop their rule sets by monitoring a user's normal network pattern.

6.6 Virtual Machines

Virtual machines can be used to prevent potentially malicious software from using the operating system for illicit actions. They typically lie between the operating system and the physical hardware. This mediation layer between the software and hardware is a powerful feature that prevents potentially malicious software from interfacing directly with real hardware.

6.7 Configuration

In this context, configuration refers to any application or operating system setting that can be adjusted to make the environment more resistant to attack. We restrict the scope of configuration settings to those that are easily changed through tools, wizards, and menus. We do not include advanced configuration typically performed by an experienced technician using undocumented features or making extensive code changes. Typical aspects of a strong configuration include tightening application settings, limiting the use of network ports, running only required services, and setting the most restrictive and granular permissions on the file system and the registry.

6.8 Anti-virus Heuristics

Traditional anti-virus products work on a "known bad" signature-based approach. They contain signatures, which are used to identify malicious code. Anti-virus vendors update these signatures on a regular basis, typically every week or as necessary. Many anti-virus products also employ heuristics in the searching for malicious code. The anti-virus product can identify new malicious code that functions in a manner similar to known worms and viruses. Heuristics allow detection of viruses and worms that may have never been studied by anti-virus researchers.

6.9 Host-based Intrusion Prevention Systems

Host-based intrusion prevention systems (HIPS) typically characterize applications by the resources they require during normal operation. Such systems usually operate from predefined rules describing what constitutes legal behavior for particular applications. These systems typically bolt policy enforcement onto the front end of crucial operating system interfaces. For instance, a HIPS might mediate Registry key creation so that worms tampering with run keys might be stopped. Such systems react to dangerous operating system requests by logging them, denying them outright, or querying the user for approval to continue the action. One possible action a HIPS can take is to terminate the offending program. This action would outright kill a worm attempting to use unauthorized system resources.

6.10 Integrity Checking

Integrity checkers make use of a trusted baseline of files on the system. They generally keep cryptographic hashes of known good instances of files so that integrity comparisons can be made at any time. Some have the ability to restore files that may have been modified by a worm.

6.11 Stackguarding

Stackguarding [25] technologies aim to make programs resistant to buffer overflow attacks.

By including special libraries or by using special compilers, the programmer produces software that cannot be remotely exploited. Stackguarding does not remove buffer overflow coding errors but prevents them from being exploited.

7 Attacks vs. Defenses

Our scheme of attack attributes provides a framework within which to match worms to defensive technologies. The attack attributes classify how worms operate, and they suggest the defenses that will be most effective. For example, many worms change Run keys within the registry (attack attribute: modifying system settings). This attribute can be defended by locking down the vulnerable registry keys (defensive technology: configuration). By matching attributes to defensive technologies for all worms that we studied, we were able to develop a fairly comprehensive defense matrix (see table 6).

The rows of the defense matrix represent the fourteen attack attributes and the columns represent defenses. The first four attributes pertain only to infection, while the remaining ten can apply to any worm life function. The intersection of an attribute and a defense represents the class of protection that that defense provides to address that attack attribute. These classes are:

- **D – Detect**. The defense can detect the attack but can do nothing to stop it. For example, file integrity checkers can detect that a file has been modified but cannot prevent the modification.

- **P – Provides Partial Protection**. Some defenses are good at preventing certain attacks, but can be subverted depending on the precise details of the attack's implementation. For example, mail servers can be configured to filter out attachments that contain executable files. This provides only partial protection against worms that trick the user because the files can reach the user through other channels besides email.

- **R – Reactive Protection**. The defense can detect and defeat the attack, but only after the attack is known. Reactive defenses are generally signature-based, such as intrusion detection systems.

- **B – Blocks Attack**. The defense effectively blocks the attack.

A blank entry indicates that the defense provides no effective protection against the attack attribute.

7.1 The Defense Matrix

Key: **B**=Blocks; **R**=Reactively Blocks; **P**=Protects partially; **D**=Detects

Attack Attribute \ Defense Attribute	Packet Filtering FW	Stateful FW	Application Proxy FW	IDS	Host FW	VM	Configuration	AV with Heuristics	HIPS	Integrity Check	Stackguarding
Exploits vulnerable network code (infection)	R	R	B	R	R		B				B
Tricks a user (infection)			B		B		P				
Exploits vulnerable configuration (infection)	B	B	B		B		B				
Exploits previously installed backdoor (infection)	B	B	B		B			B			
Changes file system							B		B	D	
Changes system settings							B		B	D	
Modifies some process							B		B		
Accesses the network	P	P	P		B				B		
Requires system privilege							B		B		B
Performs anomalous queries							B		B		
Invokes crucial APIs						B			B		
Causes network flooding	B	B	B		B				B		
Slows local system									P		
Contains worm signatures			P	P				B			

Table 6 - Detailed Defense Matrix

30

7.2 Observations About the Defense Matrix

Ideally, worms should be prevented from infecting a system. The defense matrix suggests that employing stackguarding technology is a logical first step. This would take care of many of the vulnerabilities exploited by worms. The matrix also indicates that firewalls provide the most comprehensive protection against the four infection-related attributes. Firewalls, however, provide very limited protection against the files that enter the system "legally" and then trick the user into infecting himself. They also cannot protect against unknown logic flaws in exposed network interfaces. Thus perimeter defenses alone are insufficient to provide full protection from worm-based attacks.

The remaining ten attack attributes seem to be best defended by host-based intrusion prevention systems and proper system configuration. These two defenses block or defend against nine of the ten non-infection attributes, and also cover 12 of the complete list of 14. HIPS and configuration work at the host application and operating system level, where worms' later life stages are carried out.

Selecting from the defenses in the matrix, it is possible to devise a multi-layered protection scheme that can counter every type of attack attribute. If the selected defensive strategy uses defenses that completely block attributes, it may be possible to block even zero-day worms.

In the sections below, we explain each column of the defense matrix and describe how each defense deals with each attack attribute.

7.2.1 Packet Filtering Firewalls

Proper firewall configuration is critical for providing effective protection. The guiding principal of firewall configuration is to block all incoming traffic except for that which is essential to the functioning of the network. Limiting the exposure of the network's interior reduces the chance that a vulnerability or backdoor on an internal machine can be remotely exploited.

Because packet-filtering firewalls make decisions based on IP addresses and port numbers, they cannot protect ports that must be left open. If an open port is used by a network service that is found to be vulnerable, it can be closed by an administrator as an interim solution at the expense of legitimate traffic.

Packet filtering firewalls can also protect poorly configured host systems. For example, a host with an uneccessary network service enabled can be protected by filtering at the firewall. Realistically, some services cannot be blocked because they are necessary. This technology can not mitigate all aspects of a poor configuration, such as running required services with higher privilege than required.

Through their logging capabilities, packet-filtering firewalls can also help to identify network flooding indicative of worm propagation. Once such an attack is identified, the firewall is capable of stopping it. This also impacts legitimate traffic attempting to pass through the firewall.

Additionally, a packet filtering firewall can block access to the external network. This offers no protection within the network protected by the firewall. Filtering outgoing traffic disrupts the normal model of network operations and is not a reasonable solution.

7.2.2 Stateful Firewalls

A stateful firewall provides the base protection of a packet filtering firewall plus it ensures that only packets associated with an internally initiated connection are allowed. This is an improved solution because it allows for filtering based on conditions rather than merely blocking or allowing certain types of traffic.

7.2.3 Application Proxy Firewalls

Application proxy firewalls are similar to the previous two technologies in that they can filter traffic based on ports and IP addresses. They also have the ability to filter traffic based on its content, which provides additional protection against worms. They can verify that all fields have valid lengths and permissible content because they understand the higher layer protocol definitions. Field length filtering can prevent overflows that exploit those fields. Content filtering can ensure that the fields have legitimate data. Using these techniques, proxy firewalls can drop packets that contain exploits or shell code.

Proxy-based solutions can be used to filter all executable attachments. This protection has its limits because renaming the attachment or encrypting the email can circumvent it. Unfortunately, strict proactive filtering limits users' ability to share legitimate non-malicious files. Application proxies offer an additional benefit when used reactively. They are able to filter emails that match known bad values; thus protecting systems from worms that gain control by tricking a user.

7.2.4 Intrusion Detection Systems

An Intrusion Detection System (IDS) can best be thought of as a combination virus scanner and network sniffer. With a few exceptions, IDS systems function in a reactive manner; only taking action after the damage has been done. This makes them good devices for alerting administrators about the presence of known malicious code or suspicious behavior that seeks to exploit vulnerable network code. They are fairly useless in detecting unknown exploits, unknown worms, and/or polymorphic worms and viruses that are capable of self-encrypting themselves to avoid signature-based detection methods.

7.2.5 Host Firewalls

Host firewalls enforce a policy defining which processes can access the network. Because of this they can block worm-spawned programs that attempt to send out packets. They can also block rogue programs that flood the network. This assumes that the process invoked by the worm is not disguised as one that can legitimately use the network.

In addition to screening outgoing connections, host firewalls can also filter incoming traffic based on protocols, IP addresses, and ports. This includes requests to backdoor ports and services that should not be exposed.

Advanced host firewalls can reactively scan for malicious signatures, usually in cooperation with anti-virus technology. While scanning incoming email, high-risk attachments can also be dropped. This protection has the same limitation as an Application Proxy Firewall - renaming the attachment or encrypting the email can circumvent it.

7.2.6 Virtual Machines

Virtual machines normally provide virtual resources to the operating system. Worms that attempt to run in such an environment can only damage the virtual resources and not the true operating system or hardware. For example, the Magistr worm would have been unable to overwrite the actual system BIOS if it was executed in a virtual machine. In this way, virtual machines protect against worms that *invoke crucial APIs,* although only those that attempt to touch the hardware. Virtual machines can also help a user recover their system, once an attack has been detected. They often have the ability to restore the system to a previous, uninfected state.

7.2.7 Configuration

A hardened configuration protects against vulnerabilities by locking down services and disabling those that are not essential.

With secure configuration, privileged accounts are only used when they are required to complete the task or run the service. If the exploited service does not require system privileges and the "principle of least privilege" has been enforced, the worm will be unable to use such advanced privileges. Setting restrictive permissions can also prevent a worm from modifying another running process or performing anomalous queries.

Hardening email applications, by specifically preventing the automatic execution of attachments, helps prevent worms that propagate through email.

Enforcing strong permissions on the file system as well as the Registry can limit the number of changes that a worm will be able to make to a system configuration. This also restricts the amount of information that worms can obtain from such a system.

Some security settings may be difficult to implement effectively because all users have a legitimate need to access certain files. Setting restrictive permissions can render them inaccessible to all users. In these circumstances, a careful balance must be made in order to give users access to exactly what they require and nothing more.

7.2.8 Anti-virus with Heuristics

Properly updated anti-virus tools can identify, quarantine, and even clean up known worms. They are also capable of performing the same types of actions against Trojan backdoor programs and other such malicious code. The downside to this approach is that anti-virus researchers must study each worm and publish signatures that can identify it. It is then upon end users to update their signature files to ensure their signature databases are up-to-date. Of course, this type of anti-virus program only protects against known threats and is unable to detect worms for which anti-virus vendors have not yet developed signatures. To help against this type of threat, most modern anti-virus products also look for heuristics. This is a set of worm or virus like code segments (code patterns that appear to be common to malicious code). While this is a good technology to have in place, worm authors who are aware of its existence and the types of patterns it is looking for can easily defeat it.

It is worth pointing out that anti-virus products typically work at the file system level, meaning that they monitor and scan files as a process accesses them. Some worms, such as CodeRed, exist only in memory and never write themselves to the file system. In essence, they do not try to maintain the control they have seized. While this behavior makes this type of worm easier to clean up, it also prevents most anti-virus products from detecting them.

7.2.9 Host-based Intrusion Prevention Systems

HIPS can mediate file system, network, registry, process, and privilege escalation requests. They can identify idiosyncrasies, such as anomalous queries or network flooding, and deny them. HIPS can also detect spikes in local system activity by watching for excessive file system activity, memory usage, or network socket allocations. Once detected, they can stop the offending processes. This is the only technology that has some ability to prevent a worm from degrading system performance.

These systems can also block access to system resources not protected by strong configuration, stop backdoors from running, and prevent malicious worm actions even if a user has been tricked into launching the worm. All this is possible because they validate specific actions. They also protect against vulnerable network code, as such programs will be restricted to performing only their expected functions.

7.2.10 Integrity Checkers

An integrity checker could detect any changes made to the *file system* by a worm. Changes that could reveal a worm's presence would be caught by these systems include the introduction of executable files, such as Trojan backdoors, and the modification of configuration files. These files are typically modified in order to allow a worm to survive through reboots. The downside of this technology is that integrity checkers are usually only run infrequently. Registry integrity checkers also exist.

7.2.11 Stackguarding

Stackguarding technology makes it extremely difficult for attackers to exploit buffer overflows, the most common type of vulnerability discovered in network code. Of the thirteen vulnerability-based infiltration vectors seen in our corpus of worms, six were buffer overflows.

Stackguarding can also prevent worms from gaining increased privileges on that system. Worms that gain control of a low-privilege account may attempt to elevate their privilege. Stackguarding can defend against this type of attack as well.

8 Case Studies: Applying Defensive Methodology

In this section, we apply our methodology of layered defense to five aggressive historical worms and demonstrate how they could have been defeated. We summarize our findings in figure 8-1 and describe each case in the following sections.

Defense / Worm	Packet Filtering FW	Stateful FW	Application Proxy FW	IDS	Host FW	VM	Configuration	AV Heuristics	HIPS	Integrity Checker	Stackguarding
YAHA			X		X		X		X	X	
SLAMMER	X	X	X	X	X		X			X	X
BUGBEAR			X		X		X		X	X	
LEAVE	X	X	X		X			X	X		
NIMDA			X	X	X		X		X	X	X

Table 7 - Summary of Case Study Results

8.1 YAHA.G

8.1.1 Infection

8.1.1.1 Description

Yaha uses two infection vectors to gain initial control of target systems. First, it tries to take advantage of an error in the way that MIME headers are processed within Internet Explorer (Microsoft email clients use Internet Explorer to process HTML mail messages). This vulnerability allows an attacker who has manipulated certain MIME headers to automatically run an attached binary file. As an alternate infection vector, Yaha can gain control of a system by tricking a user into clicking on an executable attachment.

8.1.1.2 Defenses

The MIME flaw exploited by Yaha could be mitigated by disabling file downloads within the Security Zones feature of Internet Explorer. There is no universal defense for the infection vector of the user clicking on an attachment. Some firewalls and mail servers are able to filter email and remove executable code and scripts. This makes the sharing of executable files via email more difficult, but would prevent this type of infection vector.

8.1.2 Survival

8.1.2.1 Description

After gaining control of a host, Yaha alters the Registry and system directory to ensure that it is run regularly. Specifically, it modifies the "HKLM\exefile\shell\open\command\default" Registry key and copies itself into the system directory. The worm may attempt to kill any host-based technologies before beginning its propagation.

8.1.2.2 Defenses

The file changes that Yaha makes to the system directory are detectable by both HIPS and integrity checkers. A HIPS could prevent the file write from succeeding, while an integrity checker, once it is run, could detect the changes. Secure configuration, through restrictive file permissions, would also stop Yaha from making file changes.

Yaha's registry changes could be prevented by either proper configuration or HIPS. The system's configuration could be changed to restrict access to certain registry keys, thus blocking the worm's attempt to access the "exefile" key. HIPS, likewise, can counter Registry modifications with a policy to prevent access to certain keys or hives.

Yaha also attempts to kill any anti-virus or host firewall program that it can find, provided that it is a version Yaha knows how to kill (as different variants of this worm attempt to disable different defense programs). Some host firewalls warn the user when they are being shut down and allow them to abort such an action; this is a good feature that could mitigate the risk of a malicious program shutting down a host-based firewall. A HIPS might also be effective in this case, as such systems are capable of detecting and preventing one process' attempts to modify or control another.

8.1.3 Propagation

8.1.3.1 Description

Yaha creates a list of target email addresses by searching through the Windows Address Book, MSN Messenger Data, ICQ data files, and other email resources. Once it has a collection of target addresses, Yaha tries to find the default SMTP server by looking in the "HKCU\Software\Microsoft\Internet Account Manager\Accounts" registry key. If no default SMTP server is found, Yaha uses a predefined external server and connects to it using the standard SMTP port (TCP port 25).

8.1.3.2 Defenses

Yaha's reconnaissance for email addresses could be prevented by a HIPS configured to spot accesses to files or registry keys containing email addresses. Likewise, tight access controls on the registry could prevent such reconnaissance. The worm's access to SMTP servers is preventable with host-based firewalls and application proxy firewalls which block unauthorized connections. A HIPS could also be set up to prevent rogue programs from issuing commands to connect to an SMTP server.

8.1.4 Payload

8.1.4.1 Description

Periodically, Yaha tries to connect to the target system www.pak.gov.pk.

8.1.4.2 Defenses

If multiple copies of Yaha run on the same network segment, a noticeable amount of network traffic is generated. This can be detected with IDSs and firewalls. If the administrator notices a URL being attacked, he could configure firewalls or a HIPS to block requests to that destination.

8.2 SLAMMER

8.2.1 Infection

8.2.1.1 Description

Slammer gains control of a system using a buffer overflow in the SQL Server Resolution Service of Microsoft's SQL Server and MSDE 2000 (a desktop data engine component that shares code within SQL Server).

8.2.1.2 Defenses

The vulnerablity exploited by Slammer was well known and a patch was available in January 2003 when the worm was released. The massive impact and rapid spread of the worm is a good indication of how few system administrators had applied the patches.

The impact of Slammer could have been greatly reduced if more systems had been properly configured. It is generally not necessary that the SQL Server Resolution Service be visible to the Internet, nor does it have to run with system privileges. If this service is not visible from the outside, Slammer cannot get in. If the service runs as a normal user, its damage is limited by operating system permissions.

A properly configured packet filtering firewall could have also stopped Slammer infection by blocking inbound packets aimed at the SQL Server Resolution Service. There is seldom a legitimate reason for the service to be accessible over the Internet.

Exploitation of the buffer overflow vulnerability in this service could have been prevented using stackguarding. Alternatively, a proxy firewall could perform a validity check on the field being overflowed by Slammer.

8.2.2 Survival

8.2.2.1 Description

Slammer resides in memory and makes no permanent changes to the Windows Registry or to system files to ensure its survival on the target machine.

8.2.2.2 Defenses

Slammer did not try to corrupt the target system. It was not defensible by host-oriented protections that look for resources being corrupted.

8.2.3 Propagation

8.2.3.1 Description

The worm propagates by generating small-sized packets that exploit the SQL Resolution Service vulnerability and sending them out indescriminately to IP address on the Internet. Slammer's aggressive propagation generated massive amounts of traffic that quickly flooded networks all over the world.

8.2.3.2 Defenses

Propagation can be stopped at network gateways with properly configured packet filtering firewalls. If the firewalls are eluded, an IDS may be able to detect packet flooding. There is little that can be done at an infected host other than disconnecting from the network, rebooting, and installing the patches.

8.2.4 Payload

8.2.4.1 Description

Slammer has no payload. The propagation of the worm itself does all the damage.

8.2.4.2 Payload

Slammer has no payload, so there is nothing to defend against.

8.3 BUGBEAR

8.3.1 Infection

8.3.1.1 Description

The Bugbear worm spreads primarily by execution of an email attachment that contains the worm. The execution may be initiated by an unsuspecting user or triggered through a vulnerability in MIME header processing code in Internet Explorer (the same flaw exploited by Yaha).

8.3.1.2 Defenses

Filtering email to remove executable attachments and disabling file downloads in the Internet Explorer Security Zone are effective countermeasures to Bugbear's infection vectors.

8.3.2 Survival

8.3.2.1 Description

Bugbear copies itself to the system directory and places itself in the startup folder so that it will be executed each time the system reboots. The RunOnce key in the Registry is set to point to Bugbear as a backup measure to ensure it is executed at system startup.

Like Yaha, Bugbear attempts to disable security software on the host computer. It also disables autodialing at various points so the user is not alerted by dialing at unusual times.

8.3.2.2 Defenses

The survival steps taken by Bugbear could be mediated via tight permissions on the Registry and filesystem. The Registry could be configured to restrict access on keys that contain email addresses. Restrictive permissions only help if the account Bugbear runs under does not normally require access.

HIPSs offer mediation that can stop Bugbear's survival functions which consist of modifications to the Registry and file system. They could also counter attempts to shutdown anti-virus and host-based firewall programs since they can screen the process-related APIs.

8.3.3 Propagation

8.3.3.1 Description

Bugbear propagates by mailing infected files as email attachments. The worm uses varying subject lines, attachment names, and destination email addresses. This makes it difficult to filter with content-checking firewalls.

In addition to using email as a propagation method, Bugbear attempts to propagate through open file shares.

8.3.3.2 Defenses

Outgoing email could be filtered by a mail server or advanced application proxy firewall that drops executable attachments.

HIPS guard against Bugbear's alternate propagation mechanism, ensuring that only legitimate processes are accessing file shares.

8.3.4 Payload

8.3.4.1 Description

Bugbear installs a backdoor that optionally listens on TCP ports 36794 and 1080. The backdoor listens for commands issued by its author. A keystroke logger is also installed on compromised machines. The keystroke logger creates files in the system directory.

8.3.4.2 Defenses

The best way to combat Bugbear's payloads is to prevent them from being installed and run. Proper configuration could lock down the directories the worm uses to install the backdoor and keylogger. HIPS could watch for system changes that initiate these payloads.

Assuming the payload components do run, packet filtering (done by any of the various types of firewalls) could prevent commands from reaching the backdoor. Unfortunately, shutting down one of the ports, 1080, disables a legitimate service and may impact the functioning of the system. If all else fails and the backdoor can be instructed from the outside, the commands the backdoor executes will likely be out-of-character and thereby be defendable by a HIPS. The keystroke logger, likewise, will perform actions that are detectable at the host.

8.4 LEAVE

8.4.1 Infection

8.4.1.1 Description

The Leave worm uses two main techniques to infect a host. Its primary method of infection is to take advantage of the SubSeven Trojan. This method of infection requires the victim to have been previously compromised by a version of SubSeven that has the backdoor component active.

Leave's secondary infection mechanism involves binding itself to an executable file. When an infected program is executed, usually by tricking a user, Leave extracts itself and infects the system.

8.4.1.2 Defenses

The primary infection vector utilizes the SubSeven Trojan. SubSeven was detectable by anti-virus software long before the appearance of the Leave worm. Had users been running up-to-date anti-virus software, they would have been free of the SubSeven Trojan and would have been immune to infection from Leave via this method. Additionally, firewalls could have been configured to block the port used by the SubSeven backdoor.

8.4.2 Survival

8.4.2.1 Description

Once Leave has penetrated a system it immediately takes steps to prevent its detection and removal. It selects common Windows applications such as Notepad and Internet Explorer and attaches itself to their executable files. Each time one of these modified programs is executed, Leave is able to reinfect the system.

Additionally, Leave modifies various Registry keys to ensure that Windows executes it on system startup. Should these Registry keys be removed, the execution of an infected application restores them.

8.4.2.2 Defenses

The survival mechanisms of the Leave worm can be mitigated through HIPSs and file system integrity checkers.

HIPSs can be used to detect and prevent Leave's attempts to modify system Registry keys. As Leave relies on Registry keys to have the operating system execute it, it will not run at startup if these keys are not present.

Leave also relies on binding itself with various commonly used programs. File system integrity checkers can immediately alert the user when a program attempts to modify other executables.

8.4.3 Propagation

8.4.3.1 Description

The original Leave worm has both an active and a passive propagation vector.

The active method of propagation involves scanning the Internet for computers infected with the SubSeven Trojan. When an infected machine is found, Leave uses the SubSeven backdoor to copy itself to the remote machine.

The applications that Leave infects when it infiltrates a system can also be used as propagation vectors. If they are executed on another computer, they infect the new system.

Later variants of the Leave worm were packaged as email attachments masquerading as patches sent by Microsoft.

8.4.3.2 Defenses

The Leave worm is extremely network aware. It scans for potential victims on the Internet. It uses the IRC, HTTP, and NTP protocols in its normal operation. It relies on the network in almost every facet of its lifecycle. A host firewall would deny it these capabilities. Should the Leave worm attempt to access any part of the network, the host-based firewall could immediately intercept this action and alert the user. Its network capabilities would be completely compromised.

8.4.4 Payload

8.4.4.1 Description

The Leave worm offers its author the ability to have near complete control of an infected machine.

After Leave ensures its survival, it synchronizes the system clock with various publicly accessible NTP (Network Time Protocol) servers. It connects to various websites and downloads a list of commands the worm author may have posted. It also connects to a private IRC channel and awaits commands sent directly from the worm creator. The commands Leave supports include the ability to modify the local file system, copy files, upload/download files, modify files, bind to alternate executables, attack new hosts, and many more. The Leave worm can function as a malicious remote-administration tool with few limitations.

8.4.4.2 Defenses

The Leave worm has no intention of destroying data on the host. In fact, it removes the SubSeven backdoor to prevent reinfection or infection by another worm. Since all command and control is accomplished via the network, a host-based firewall would sever Leave's tie to the outside world. A HIPS would be able to mediate the system changes if the backdoor commands were remotely invoked.

8.5 NIMDA

8.5.1 Infection

8.5.1.1 Description

Nimda has four infection vectors. Its primary infection technique is to exploit the same MIME header parsing vulnerability in Internet Explorer that was used in Yaha and Bugbear. In other scenarios it may try to trick a user into manually executing an attachment or into downloading a file off of the web. The fourth infection vector is the remote exploitation of a buffer overflow in the Microsoft WWW server IIS (Internet Information Services).

8.5.1.2 Defenses

The MIME header parsing vulnerability results in attachments being executed without user action. This vulnerability can be eliminated with proper patching policies. Attachment filtering, done at the mail server or firewall, could also remove any such attachments before they reach the client.

Disabling file downloads in Internet Explorer Security Zones could prevent clients from accidentally downloading any content from an infected IIS server.

If IIS was compiled with stackguarding, the buffer overflow within IIS would have been unexploitable, and this infection vector would have been rendered ineffective.

8.5.2 Survival

8.5.2.1 Description

Upon infection Nimda takes numerous steps to ensure that it cannot be removed. To help hide its presence, Nimda overwrites system applications such as mmc.exe (the Microsoft Management Console) in the Windows directory. It then will scan for Microsoft Word documents and create malicious DLL files (containing a copy of the worm) in the directories the documents are found. It will change a user's preferences to not show known file extensions or hidden files so that the malicious DLLs will not be displayed.

To make sure that the worm is executed on startup, Nimda will modify Registry settings. It will also modify configuration files such as system.ini. It will also register itself as a system service so that it will be able to run even when no user is logged in.

Nimda will create open network shares for all drives on the infected computer. Finally, Nimda will also create users that have enhanced privileges on the infected machine. It will give the guest account Administrator privileges.

8.5.2.2 Defenses

The survival mechanisms of the Nimda worm can be mitigated through HIPSs and file system integrity checkers.

HIPSs can deny Nimda's attempts to modify, create, and/or delete system files and registry settings. They can also prevent a worm from creating unsafe user accounts with unnecessary privileges, causing gaps in the security posture. Finally, a HIPS can detect Nimda's attempts to access parts of the registry and file systems and deny such accesses.

File system integrity checkers can alert users to the corruption of core system programs and configuration files modified by Nimda.

8.5.3 Propagation

8.5.3.1 Description

When Nimda attempts to propagate to other machines, it has a variety of methods at its disposal. The most basic propagation technique is that Nimda will send a copy of itself to a harvested email address hoping the remote user will be vulnerable to its MIME header parsing exploit or be tricked into executing the attachment.

Nimda also has the ability to search network shares for Microsoft Word documents and create malicious DLL files that will be loaded by Microsoft Word when the documents are opened. If the user opening the document is on a remote machine, they have now infected their computer as well. Nimda also copies itself to network shares in the hope that remote users will execute them.

Since Nimda probes for vulnerable IIS servers, it may use the buffer overflow exploit to propagate to such a server. The remote server would then be infected as well. IIS servers infected with Nimda will attempt to send clients copies of the Nimda worm when they request content.

8.5.3.2 Defenses

Most of Nimda's propagation techniques involve requests for network access. Whether these requests are to send infectious emails or scan for vulnerable IIS servers, a host-based firewall could prevent these actions.

As for the modification of files on network shares, a HIPS could detect this suspicious behavior as well as prevent network share scanning and modification of system files.

8.5.4 Payload

8.5.4.1 Description

After Nimda has infected a machine, it begins executing its payload. Every ten days, Nimda will harvest email addresses from the local machine and begin mass mailing those addresses. These emails have an attachment that contains the worm as well as the MIME header parsing vulnerability exploit. Nimda will utilize it's own SMTP engine to send mail directly to a mail server, bypassing the need for an email client. Nimda will issue DNS MX requests to identify mail servers.

When Nimda copies itself to remote IIS servers, it will start a TFTP (Trivial File Transfer Protocol) server to assist in its propagation function.

8.5.4.2 Defenses

Nimda will run its own SMTP engine, perform DNS lookups, and start a TFTP (Trivial File Transfer Protocol) server. Since each of these services requires network access, a host firewall could deny their network access requests.

References

[1] The Worm Information Center, http://www.networm.org/faq

[2] CERT Coordination Center, http://www.cert.org

[3] F-Secure Virus Info Center, http://www.f-secure.com/virus-info

[4] Kaspersky Labs Virus Encylopedia, http://www.viruslist.com

[5] Network Associates AVERT Virus Information Library, http://vil.nai.com

[6] Sophos Virus Information, http://www.sophos.com/virusinfo

[7] Symantec Security Response, http://securityresponse.symantec.com/avcenter

[8] Trend Micro Virus Encylopedia, http://www.trendmicro.com/vinfo

[9] Virus Bulletin, http://www.virusbtn.com/resources/viruses/index.xml

[10] MITRE Common Vulnearbilities cve.mitre.org

[11] Microsoft Security Bulletins, http://www.microsoft.com/technet/security

[12] Symantec Security Response Glossary,
http://securityrespone.symantec.com/avcenter/refa.html

[13] CAIDA analysis of Code Red, http://www.caida.org/analysis/security/code-red

[14] Eeye Blaster Analysis, http://www.eeye.com/Research/Advisories/AL20030811.html

[15] D. Moore, C. Shannon, k claffy, "Code Red: a case study on the spread and victims of an Internet worm"

[16] J. Van Hoogstraten, "Blasting Windows: An Analysis of the W32/Blaster Worm",
http://www.giac.org/practical/GCIH/John_VanHoogstraten_GCIH.pdf

[17] E. Manrique, "An Analysis of W32.Bugbear and the Technical and Procedural Controls Needed for Protection", http://www.giac.org/practical/GCIH/Edmundo_Manrique_GCIH.pdf

[18] A. Marinescu, "An Analysis of Simile", http://www.securityfocus.com/infocus/1671

[19] P. Ferrie, "WHO? WHAT? WHERE? SWEN?", http://pferrie.tripod.com/swen.pdf

[20] P. Ferrie, "Klez", http://toronto.virusbtn.com/magazine/archives/200207/klez.xml

[21] Max Vision, "Lion Internet Worm Analysis", http://www.whitehats.com/library/worms/lion

[22] Max Vision, "Ramen Internet Worm Analysis",
http://www.whitehats.com/library/worms/ramen

[23] D. Moore, C. Shannon, G.M. Voelker, S. Savage, "Internet Quarantine: Requirements for Containing Self-Propagating Code", *Infocom 2003*

[24] S. Staniford, V. Paxson, N. Weaver, "How to 0wn the Internet in Your Spare Time" in Proceedings of he 11 USENIX Security Symposium, San Francisco, CA, Aug. 2002

[25] C. Cowan, C. Pu, D. Maier, H. Hinton, J. Walpole, P. Bakke, S. Beattie, A. Grier, P. Wagle, Q, Zhang, "StackGuard: Automatic Adaptive Detection and Prevention of Buffer-Overflow Attacks"

[26] E. Spafford, "Computer Viruses as Artificial Life"

[27] D. Chess, S. White, "An Undetectable Computer Virus"

[28] J. Nazario, J. Anderson, R. Wash, C. Connelly, "The Future of Internet Worms", Crimelabs Research, http://www.crimelabs.net

[29] P. K. Singh, "A Physiological Decomposition of Virus and Worm Programs"

[30] Tripwire Integrity Assurance Company, http://www.tripwire.com

[31] D. Moore, V. Paxson, S. Savage, C. Shannon, S. Staniford, V. Weaver, "The Spread of the Sapphire/Slammer Worm", http://www.silicondefense.com/research/slammer